All That Is
(and All That Will Ever Be)

DAVID JOHN BLACK

BALBOA.
PRESS

A DIVISION OF HAY HOUSE

Balboa Press books may be ordered through booksellers or by contacting:

Balboa Press
A Division of Hay House
1663 Liberty Drive
Bloomington, IN 47403
www.balboapress.com.au
1 (877) 407-4847

Because of the dynamic nature of the Internet, any web addresses or
links contained in this book may have changed since publication and
may no longer be valid. The views expressed in this work are solely those
of the author and do not necessarily reflect the views of the publisher,
and the publisher hereby disclaims any responsibility for them.

The author of this book does not dispense medical advice or prescribe the use
of any technique as a form of treatment for physical, emotional, or medical
problems without the advice of a physician, either directly or indirectly. The
intent of the author is only to offer information of a general nature to help
you in your quest for emotional and spiritual well-being. In the event you use
any of the information in this book for yourself, which is your constitutional
right, the author and the publisher assume no responsibility for your actions.

Any people depicted in stock imagery provided by Thinkstock are
models, and such images are being used for illustrative purposes only.
Certain stock imagery © Thinkstock.

Printed in the United States of America.

ISBN: 978-1-4525-2595-2 (sc)
ISBN: 978-1-4525-2596-9 (e)

Balboa Press rev. date: 10/28/2014

Dedicated
to
The One
I love.

Preface

Revealed to me, were the following Truths,
whilst I was on The Mountain.

Note

This book is to be pondered in the heart,
reflected upon, contemplated or meditated on –
not just skimmed from cover to cover.

The book can be read progressively and
as the reader comes across each saying
that they don't understand,
they can put the book down,
take a long walk, or do some gardening,
or sit in meditation,
and by just having that *one* question, like
'what does *this* saying mean for me?',
or 'how does *this* saying apply to my life?',
a question of this kind,
on the back of their mind,
they then just allow the answer to be revealed to them –
one way or another,
in what is known as an 'a–ha' moment.
And, if they are a person who honors their feelings,
they will know by the way they feel in the moment,
that the answer is the Truth for themselves.

In addition, the more discerning reader will
notice a progression from lesser awareness to
Greater Awareness throughout the work.

Also,
take note of the capitalization throughout.

$\mathcal{O}$nce we make a start,
we are shown The Way.

We are free to accept,
or not to accept.

$\mathcal{W}$e are <u>only</u>
who we,
<u>perceive</u> ourself
to be.

$\mathcal{W}$e are all teachers,
by the way we live our lives.

A mistake,
is not a mistake,
if we learn from it.

$\mathscr{L}$ife is a remembrance
of who we <u>truly</u> are.

$\mathcal{O}$ur labyrinth
is thoroughly known.

$\mathcal{S}$earch within.

$\mathcal{A}$bsolutely <u>nothing</u>
happens by co–incidence.

*C*o–incidence,
is when The All
just chooses
to remain anonymous.

*Follow
the connections.*

$\mathcal{D}$evelop
in the direction
of <u>least</u> resistance.

$\mathcal{T}$he whole world is
the Temple of The All.

$\mathcal{I}$t takes <u>all</u> kinds to make a world –
for without our differences,
we just wouldn't be the same.

*I*f we are to live
in this world together,
we'll just have to learn to get along.

*A*lways remember,
that people are weakest
on what they put out,
until they come to Awareness.

$\mathcal{W}$e are to live,
as though our word is our life –
if we don't keep our word,
we don't keep our life.

That which gives us
the greatest pleasure,
is that which causes us
the greatest pain.

$\mathcal{O}$nly hurt people,
hurt people.

The one who hurts us the most,
might just be our greatest teacher.

*T*hose who anger us –
control us.

$\mathcal{U}$nderneath our anger,
lay a fear,
of either –
losing something,
or in the very least,
failing to gain something.

The more we push away our fear,
the more it comes back upon us –
with uncontrollable and terrifying fury.

*W*hat we resist,
persists.

$\mathcal{W}$e keep getting it,
until we 'get' it!

*I*f nothing changes –
guess what?

Nothing changes!

$\mathcal{T}$he only <u>real</u> competition,
is with ourself.

When it comes to doing
our 'inner–work',
there's no rush –
but hurry up!

*W*hat we do in the world of work,
is the 'inner–work'
we could, not should,
be doing for ourself.

There's a big difference,
between putting the effort in –
and trying too hard.

$\mathcal{T}$he more effort we put in,
the greater the rewards will be.

$\mathcal{B}$e not a 'dog's body',
but be a God–body.

$\mathcal{B}$y constantly trying
to solve other people's problems,
we're avoiding
solving our own.

How can we save others,
if we can't even,
save ourselves?

When we do b–lame,
we are being lame,
but when we do respons–ability,
we are able to respond.

$\mathcal{B}$e not attached,
to other people's outcomes.

$\mathcal{F}$riendships and relationships,
are the mirrors in which
we discover ourself.

To have a relationship
with others,
first,
we must have
a relationship with ourself.

$\mathcal{W}$e never start
dealing with a problem,
until we give that problem,
it's <u>correct</u> name.

*O*ur life's drama
conspires to make us feel
those negative emotions
repressed since childhood.
The key to freedom,
is just to feel them clearly,
experience them
and then, let them go.
For when an issue
loses its emotional voltage on us,
it ceases to be an issue.

*When we go into
our childhood wound,
we discover
our lifetime's treasure.*

*J*ust accept,
what has been in the past –
and let go.

$\mathcal{W}$e are forgiven,
as we have forgiven.

Forgiveness is the key,
which leads to acceptance.

$\mathcal{L}$ove,
holds no grievances.

$\mathcal{B}$ehold others,
in their perfection.

*J*oy and happiness,
are the unmistakable sign
of the presence of The Divine.

There is no point
in us being
so highly spiritual,
that we are
no earthly good.

If we are
in the physical body,
we still have
work to do.

We live inside the body,
but we are not the body,
just like our body
lives inside a house,
but it's not the house.

$\mathcal{T}$ruly,
we are spiritual beings,
having a physical experience.

$\mathcal{T}$houghts <u>are</u> energy.

The things we are attached to
in the physical,
keep us in the physical.

When we release our 'baggage'
and all of our attachments
to the physical,
we become
a star in the sky.

$\mathcal{A}$nd what does a star do?

A star shines The Light
for others to see,
in the 'darkness' (of ignorance).

$\mathcal{W}$e don't need
as many things,
as we think we need.

*I*n Truth,
<u>nothing</u> can be lost
in the non–physical.

$\mathcal{I}$t's not the more we get,
the more we get –
it's the more we give up,
the more we 'get'.

$\mathcal{D}$evelop an attitude
of suitable gratitude.

$\mathcal{H}$onor
the unmerited Love of The All,
that is bestowed upon you.

$\mathcal{T}$he journey of healing,
is becoming whole.

For us to become whole,
we embrace our inner,
opposite–sexed energy.

$\mathcal{T}$o be whole,
means to include
everything and everyone,
with no exception.

Say "YES"
to All of Life!

*W*hat our mind
knows as paradox,
our heart
knows as Truth.

*W*hen we are awake,
we are asleep,
and when we are asleep,
we are our most awake.

The Mystic's Prayer:

Lead me
from the darkness to The Light,
from illusion to Reality,
from death to Immortality.

*W*e're not doing it on our own –
because we're not on our own.

*E*veryday,
be mindful,
of the need to pray.

*A*lways ask The All,
in the affirmative,
as though,
it's already been received,
by using the words
"Thank you for…"

$\mathcal{A}$sk The All,
then, allow your angels,
to bring you
the Message from The All.

$\mathcal{N}$othing,
can disturb
the deep peace
of our soul.

𝒜hhh, what peace,
there is in silence!

$\mathcal{I}$t's in the silence,
that we hear
Our Still, Small Voice.

All the answers,
lay within.

*A*ll Awareness,
starts with The Self.

*M*editate –
and believe no one.

*O*ur meditation,
doesn't take the place of our prayer;
our meditation,
is the fruit of our prayer.

$\mathscr{W}$hat is meditation,
if not the awareness of Awareness?

*I*t's <u>not</u> about doing –
it's about being.

*B*e still,
and acknowledge –
I am The All.

$\mathcal{B}$e calm and realize,
The Oneness –
which is You.

$\mathcal{B}$e All
that You can be.

*A*chieve
the sense of Oneness,
which You
<u>know</u> to be true.

*B*e at One,
with the unifying force
of Universal Awareness.

$\mathcal{I}$t's not about thinking –
it's about <u>not</u> thinking.

Our own conception
of The All,
is the last obstacle to overcome,
in 'seeing' The All.

The quickest way of knowing
the Unknown,
is to let go
of the known.

*I*n Truth,
there is <u>no</u> time,
and
there is <u>no</u> space.

$\mathcal{I}$n Truth,
there is <u>only</u>
this Present Moment;
there is <u>only</u>
this Eternal Now.

*I*n Truth,
there is <u>no</u> separation.

$\mathcal{A}$s Above, so Below –
as Within, so Without.

*W*hen We are
at One with Ourself,
We are
At One with The Universe.

$\mathcal{W}$hen We are in Awareness,
We of Ourself, do nothing.

*T*hy Will,
<u>and</u> My Will,
be done.

When We're all speaking,
with Our One True Voice,
We are all singing,
The Uni–Verse
(The One Song).

$\mathcal{W}$e are never alone –
We are Always All One.

*W*herever We are,
The All is.

$\mathcal{I}$t's not about being –
it's about <u>not</u> being.

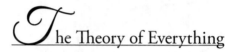he Theory of Everything

$$1 = \infty$$

$\mathcal{A}$ll is One.

Interview With David John Black

What are the professional or lifestyle credentials that make David particularly well suited to record the sayings in *All That Is*?

By age 34, David had lost his career, a house, a relationship, his car, good health, best friends, and doubted his own sanity. But, because he was working to help other people, he didn't understand why his own life was in total ruin, when he believed he was being such a 'good' person, so he began asking the question, "Why me?" In 1995, he had an experience, known to the mystics throughout the millennia, as a 'Dark Night of the Soul' (which is not to be confused with manic depression). He then started having experiences that he hadn't had before, which he pondered in his heart, or contemplated, or reflected upon what the learning was from each of the experiences. During 1997 – 2001, he camped in a tent and a trailer (caravan) and by using the technique of 'ask and receive', had a series of 'a–ha' moments, (aka 'light–bulb' moments). Not knowing where all of this was leading, one by one, he recorded the answers in this book, which have lead to the Awareness he lives with today.

Why did David record the sayings in the book? Is there any 'back story' that inspired him to record them?

After he started having experiences and reflecting on, pondering or contemplating their meaning, (rather than rationally deducing them), he realized that he was on to something *really* B–I–G. Out of his passion, he started delivering classes to small groups of people and some participants asked him to write a book, which he resisted for many a year, until a student said that she'd love to have a little book of his sayings to carry around with her. In an instant, he knew that was do–able, and so published this collection of insightful one–liners that he'd received as answers. So in short, this little book has been called for. It has universal appeal, as it can help adults of *all* ages and of *all* cultures live their *best possible* life – by being at one with themselves, and so all others, ***and*** by being at One with The Oneness of All of Life.

Which does David feel is more interesting to others – himself or the book, and why?

Both – David is not separate from the book and the book is not separate from him. In order to live an authentic life as an inspirational speaker, David has to 'walk the talk' or 'practice what he preaches' if you like. As he points out, "We are to live as though our word is our life. If we don't keep our word, we don't keep our life!"

The meaning of the sayings can best be rendered with the spoken word and a few diagrams for the audience to 'get it' in the moment. The sayings in the book have come using the technique of 'ask and receive' or what science calls the Lateral Thinking Process (aka 'thinking outside the box'). The answers have come in all different ways – intuitively, or in meditation, or from other people's words or questions, or from opening a book or newspaper and reading where his eyes first glanced, or from switching on the radio and hearing the song which was playing, etc. Being a person who honors his feelings, he knew by the way he felt in the moment, that the answer to each question was the Truth.

What is the most controversial aspect of David's message?

To many people who only use the logical–rational aspect of mind, the sayings in the book will appear to be contradictory or paradoxical, but rather than just dismissing them out of hand, if the reader ponders them in his/her heart, or reflects upon, or contemplates them and uses the intuitive aspect of mind (aka the Lateral Thinking Process), the Truth of the sayings will become apparent. As David says, "What our mind knows as paradox, our heart knows as Truth".

To discover the Truth in each of the sayings for oneself is truly an exhilarating process – leaving the reader thinking/feeling to themselves, 'Geez, I wish I'd thought of that!'

What themes in the book are relevant to today's news topics, society, or life in general?

Over time, the problem has arisen, that so many of us have learnt to live *so* unnaturally – it's like, we've *forgotten* who we are and what the *purpose* of Life on Earth is! The answers to Life's big questions – who we are, why we're here, and what we're meant to be doing, allow us to *live on purpose*, or *live in awareness*, or *live consciously*, or *live mindfully*, (choose the phrase with which you're most comfortable). Imagine if you will, if everyone living on Planet Earth understood that "Life is a *remembrance* of who we truly are". Just imagine how dramatically better human life on Earth would be. Imagine for a moment, what it would be like, if everyone understood the *emotional purpose* as to why we:

- do this job for a living and not some other job;
- believe this and don't believe that (aka motivated reasoning or confirmation bias);
- have these addictions and not other addictions;
- do this and don't do that;
- say this and don't say that;
- wear these clothes but not other clothes;
- laugh at these jokes and can't laugh at other jokes;
- like these people and not those people;
- listen to this music and not that music;
- read these books and not those books;
- watch these movies and not those movies;
- play these sports and not those sports; and so on.

When we can understand the reason why we feel drawn to any of these behaviors or beliefs, it allows us to have *true* freedom, that is, the freedom to *choose* our emotional reactions, or motivations, in *any* given situation. (Think about it! – *not* to get out of bed of a morning – is a *choice* to stay in bed, if we understand the *emotional purpose* that it's serving for us, in the moment). In understanding ourselves better as a person, (as it's said, 'what makes us tick'), we can understand all other people better.

And why is *this* so important?

It's important because, having mental clarity, in turn leads to clear communication, which then leads to less confusion / misunderstandings and therefore, less conflict, whether it be within ourselves (in the sense, of the heart versus the head), in our intimate relationship, with other family members, in our neighborhood, with our work colleagues, in our government, or in our society as a whole. As David says, "When We all speak with Our One True Voice, We are all singing The Uni–Verse (The One Song)." In other words, we are all in harmony – within ourselves, with each other, within a society, living on The Earth, and with The All, (however we conceive that to be).

Is *All That Is* based on David's own life experience in any way?

Each of the sayings, or learnings in the book have resulted from David having an experience of life and then pondering in his heart, or wondering about, or contemplating, why he was having that particular experience, in other words, what was the meaning of the experience. So the sayings in the book are all from his life experience. Some people have remarked that the sayings in the book are answers specific to himself. But what they have failed to realize is, that on Christmas Day in 1995, he asked quite literally, to be shown (not told), a way that he could impart the meaning of what he was experiencing to others.

What specific problems or challenges do readers of *All That Is* face which the book can resolve?

Do a test! Ask people who you know what their favorite color is and you'll get answers like 'red', 'blue', 'green', 'yellow', and so on, or 'I don't know'. For those that can nominate a color, then ask them the follow–up question: 'Why is that your favorite color?' Most of the time, they'll say 'I don't know', or 'I just like the color.' There's nothing bad or wrong with a person not knowing why a certain color is their favorite. But it reveals a lack of self–awareness. And just as they don't know why a certain color is their favorite, they 'sleepwalk' through their life continually making decisions or behaving in ways without knowing why they're saying this or doing that. The problem arises that their habitual ways of thinking and behaving, may not lead to what they want to experience in life – the wanted outcomes of joy and happiness, good health, peace of mind, harmonious relationships and material abundance.

Amongst people generally, there is a basic lack of understanding as to who we are as individuals, why we are here and what we are meant to be doing. The conflict between our ego–personality and our Higher Self (also called the

Superconscious Mind) leads to our lack of understanding Self and therefore others, our inability to express our emotions openly and honestly in the moment (i.e. assertively) which can result in confusion / misunderstandings and ultimately disagreements / arguments / conflict. This process unfolds on an individual level and a societal level.

By contrast, when we are in Awareness, we can have the presence of mind to ask for an answer to a question, then with patience allow the answer to unfold, and then have the courage to take the required action, confident in the knowing that the action is correct to achieve the wanted outcomes of joy and happiness, good health, peace of mind, harmonious relationships and material abundance.

What is the one thing that David wants readers to learn or take away from the sayings in *All That Is*?

Because, as he says, "Absolutely *nothing* happens by coincidence!", readers are inspired to remember, that *every* single moment of our day, *every* day of our lives, can be pregnant with, or informed by, an experience of The Oneness of All of Life. Simply by refraining from anticipating the future, or dwelling on the past, and maintaining the presence of mind, to *stay* in The Now and observing and reflecting upon what's *actually* going on around us, we can receive helpful information. When we *silently remark* to ourselves (after having the same thing pop up at us, over and over again) – there's that number again, or that colour, or that person's name, or that object, or that person who reminds us of someone we know, or that same tree or plant, or that same bird or animal again; OR, when something completely 'out of the blue', something so *totally* unusual, happens to us – instead of just dismissing the experience with 'oh, that's *just* a co–incidence', that's when to reflect upon, contemplate, or ponder, the *meaning* of that experience, in order to get the learning, so we can take another step on our Path, or to move forward with our lives, or to grow as a person, and then, to be able to help all others walk their own Paths, on their own journey of Self Discovery, on their own Sacred Quest. The further we go on our Path, the more benefit we can be to others.

What was the most challenging part about writing this book?

As has been said by another, (and paraphrased here), "the best things in life can't be spoken; the second best things are misunderstood and the third best things are what we talk about." Most of us, at one time or another have had experiences for which there are no words – words simply cannot do them justice! Think about it. Try describing to someone how exquisitely subtle it is to be awoken, before dawn, by the brightness of the Morning Star. Or, try describing all the feelings, sensations, expressions and thoughts had by those present at the birth of a new–born infant. Or perhaps, try explaining the vague, seemingly non–sensical, symbolic imagery of a dream one had last night.

As most people are probably already aware, if someone understands something well – they're able to explain it simply! It's been a long, arduous, painstaking and challenging journey for David to surrender himself to a Higher Awareness, allow himself to have the experiences, to have the presence of mind to ask for the words, to have the patience to allow the learnings from each experience to come, and now to have recorded them in *All That Is*.

About The Author

Born under The Crux, on the world's largest island *and* smallest continent, David John Black, an author and inspirational speaker, whose first name means 'the beloved', took his first breath on the 13th day of Spring – the number 13 being symbolic of Transformation and Spring being the season of Rebirth. His grandparents, who raised him, lived in house number 13. His mother remarried on the 13th day of the month. He turned 13 years of age on Black Friday. His first love lived in house number 13. His only relationship partner's birthday was the 13th of the month. In 1995, he had the life–changing experience of a 'Dark Night of The Soul' and began having experiences, so he asked "Show me in a way that I can impart this to others." In a series of 'a–ha' moments, (aka 'light–bulb' moments), the mathematical statement $1 = \infty$, expressing The Theory of Everything (TOE), which physicists had been searching for since the 1900's, was revealed to him. Also, in 1997, he heard 'The Music of The Spheres', was awoken by the brightness of the Morning Star and met his essence twin (aka twin flame). Whilst on The Mountain*, he quite literally, allowed the meaning of life – who we truly are, why we are here and

---

* Hint: all the really B–I–G stuff happens in either The Wilderness, The Forest, or on The Mountain.

what we are meant to be doing, to be revealed to him – and now to us.

Postscript: In 2013, he turned 52 years of age (4 x 13), on Friday the 13th.

Reviews

"The lyricist Maynard James Keenan from my favorite band *'Tool'*, an American spiritual art rock band, said "if I cannot heal from my art, how can it heal you?" I feel the same when I read this book – it has the ability to *heal* people, to guide them to make wiser decisions involving their own life and their relationship with others, which is highly commendable and *necessary* in fact in such a superficial, chaotic world. I respect you David … you are 'Rocky Balboa with wings' – please keep writing." – Suez Anwar, India.

"This book is just over 1200 words long, but contrary to what logic dictates its size is subjective. It is short in the sense that you can read it all in two minutes, but you can meditate on each of its sentences for a whole lifetime, therefore making the book of infinite length." – Pedro Barrento, Portugal, author of *'The Prince and the Singularity - A Circular Tale'*.

"I liked it for its shortness and concentrated wisdom in every single sentence. Some sentences become clear only after several repetitions. Greatly activates my radiant thinking … gonna read it again a bit later, to see if my perception changes over time." – Mikhail Gamov, Kazakhstan.

"Great book – very spiritual. This isn't a book that you can just mindlessly skim through, each quote is meant to be pondered for as long as it takes. I know I'll be going back through this book many times in the future." – Michael Joyce, USA.

"David understands the virtue of adhering to a minimalist aesthetic in matters of the spirit. That does not mean the book lacks substance however. Quite the opposite is true, as each page contains words of wisdom able to be contemplated deeply and seriously. Treat this book like an espresso shot of spirituality; one small dose nourishes the soul for an entire day." – Paul LeBlanc, USA.

"Thank you David for this book which makes me think deeply about life. It brought me self improvement about my daily way of thinking." – Guillaume Mansoux, France.

"I read this booklet, then found I had to go back and consider each page separately; be in my space, so to speak. Each page elicits contemplation which takes me quite deep. There are a few quotes that don't ring the right bells, however, I'll most definitely be going back to those, on a 'pick–a–page–and–just–go–there' style to fully appreciate the depth of each saying and it's meaning to me." – Thomas Rex, Australia.

"Made me think about what 'it really is all about' – thoughtful, deep writing. Thank you!" – Michel Schreck, Switzerland.

"When I really focused on the sayings presented in the book, I discovered there truly is a very deep and profound meaning behind each and every quote. I felt that there was a deep wisdom, and even some form of divinity in the quotes. Truly, an insightful book if you allow it to be." – Steve Yetman, USA.